HOW TO HIRE AN EXECUTOR

FOR YOUR LOVED ONE'S ESTATE OR YOUR WILL

ANTHONY S. PARK

DEDICATION

*For everyone who's asked me what I do for a living,
and walked away thinking I'm a funeral director*

THANK YOU FOR YOUR FEEDBACK

Hearing directly from you, the reader, is the best way for me to make these books as useful as possible.

Please share how this book has helped you, or any suggestions for how I can make it better. You can email me at executor@anthonyspark.com or call me at 212-401-2990.

I thank you in advance for your feedback.

Best,

Anthony

CONTENTS

INTRODUCTION

There are two reasons I wrote this book:

First, people have no idea what I do for a living. Not even my friends and family.

I was chatting with a dad from my daughter's school, and he politely asked what I do. As usual, I started with, "I help families settle the final affairs when someone dies," and mentioned the legal, tax, and other things I handle.

Soon, a third parent joined our conversation. The dad I had been chatting with confidently introduced me: "Oh, this is Anthony, he's a funeral director." Sigh.

From now on I'll just carry a few copies of this book with me and hand them out.

Second, most folks still have no idea that hiring a professional executor is a thing. But once they find out — especially if they've ever been guilted into being an executor — they are **thrilled** to learn this option exists.

This is my attempt to help spread the word, so families realize they don't have to draw straws or play rock-paper-scissors to avoid the thankless job of executor.

WHO IS THIS BOOK FOR?

This book is for anyone who's had a death in the family but doesn't have the time—or the desire—to take charge of settling the estate. Here are just a few common situations we see:

1. Hans died overseas but owned some U.S. assets. His heirs need help collecting their inheritance.

2. Aunt May died in New York, but all her heirs live abroad and need help settling her New York estate.

3. Greg died in New York, but his siblings are scattered across the U.S., and no one particularly wants to keep flying back and forth.

This book is also for anyone doing their own estate planning (good for you, very responsible) and thinking about naming a professional executor to settle the estate.

A BRIEF OUTLINE

In Chapter 1, **What Is an Executor?**, I'll review the basics, including an executor's responsibilities, powers, and duties.

In Chapters 2 and 3 I'll describe who usually ends up being the executor and what goes wrong when your estate has a suboptimal executor,

In Chapter 4 you'll learn what a professional executor is, and the pros and cons of using attorneys versus banks as your executor. In Chapter 5, **Why Appoint a Professional Executor?**, you'll see how a professional may solve the problems caused by an amateur executor.

In Chapters 6 through 8, I'll get into the details of **How to Hire a Professional Executor**, how much you'll pay in **Professional Executor Fees**, and answers to the most common FAQs.

Lastly, in Chapter 9 I'll tell you about my own professional executor practice, and **How to Work With Us**.

Let's get started.

CHAPTER 1

WHAT IS AN EXECUTOR?

MOST PEOPLE THINK of the executor as just the person who settles someone's final affairs, but that really doesn't do justice to the job. The executor navigates a complex set of legal, financial, and even emotional situations in order to close an estate.

For the purposes of this book, we'll use "executor" to mean anyone legally appointed to settle an estate, but It's important to understand the different titles that may apply to the job. An executor is someone who is named in a valid will, accepts the role, and is approved by the court. An administrator is someone appointed to settle the estate when there is no valid will.

There's also a third type of executor—the ancillary executor —who settles parts of the estate that are outside the primary executor's local jurisdiction.

EXAMPLE: Mssr. Toulon was a French citizen who died in France but owned an apartment in New York for business. The primary executor of Mssr. Toulon's estate lived in Paris, so he appointed an ancillary executor in New York to handle the sale of the property and file the appropriate U.S. tax returns.

Finally, an administrator c.t.a. is someone appointed by the heirs to execute the estate when the executor named in the will declines to serve.

EXAMPLE: Margo's mother named her as executor in her will. After Margo moved to Canada with her husband several years later, her mother didn't update her will to name a local executor. When her mother died, Margo declined to serve as the long-distance executor. So, the heirs appointed a local attorney to serve as administrator c.t.a. and settle the estate.

If you're serving as the executor of an estate, here's what you can expect to do:

Liquidate estate assets

The executor arranges the sale of houses, cars, and other property as required by the needs of the estate. He also finds all bank and brokerage accounts and transfers their balances into a separate estate account opened by him for that purpose. If there are owed wages or rental income, he arranges to transfer that to the estate as well, keeping meticulous records of every transaction.

If there are business interests, artwork, collectibles, or other unusual assets, the executor arranges appraisals and unravels any issues affecting their sale.

Negotiate and settle debts

The executor identifies any outstanding debts and negotiates settlements where possible. This includes things such as final cell phone bills, medical bills, credit card debt, personal loans, student loans, tax and other types of liens, and any other debts that turn up in the probate process.

File appropriate tax returns and pay applicable taxes

In addition to filing the decedent's final tax return, the executor must also file any missing returns from prior years. This happens more often than you would think, especially if the deceased was ill for a long period of time. In some cases, the estate is also required to file its own return.

Distribute the proceeds from the estate

When all the expenses and debts are settled, the executor pays out the remaining money to the heirs, according to either the deceased's will or state inheritance laws if there is no valid will.

Contrary to a common misconception, executors **do not** decide who inherits or how much each heir gets—executors must follow either the will or the state inheritance law.

THE EXECUTOR'S RESPONSIBILITIES, POWERS, AND DUTIES

Executors must be duly appointed by the court before they can act on behalf of the estate. In other words, being named in a will doesn't automatically confer legal powers on the executor. But once the court formally appoints the executor, she essentially has final say over the disposition of the estate.

Here's a look at some of an executor's legal powers, duties, and responsibilities:

Make funeral arrangements. If the decedent has no close family members, or the immediate family lives overseas, the executor has the authority to arrange a funeral.

EXAMPLE: Mrs. Kim died in her home in New Jersey; her only surviving relative was her elder sister, who lived in Korea. The elder sister asked the executor to handle Mrs. Kim's arrangements since she was too ill herself to travel to New Jersey to manage them on her own.

Liquidate assets. It's not the executor's job to act as a financial advisor—the executor should sell any stocks, bonds, and other liquid assets as soon as he has authority over the estate in order to preserve their value at the time the person died.

Executors usually sell all personal property—cars, furniture, jewelry, collectibles—unless there's a bequest in the will. And even then, the executor may still need to sell property bequeathed to an heir to pay the estate's debts.

EXAMPLE: Eitan's grandfather had a valuable sports card collection, which he left to Eitan in his will. However, when the executor was settling the estate, he uncovered a massive tax lien that could only be paid by selling off most of the assets in the estate, including the card collection. Unfortunately, Eitan only received a fraction of the cash value of the sports cards at settlement.

Liquidating assets is a challenge, even if you live in the same general area as the deceased. Doing it long-distance is virtually impossible without a reliable local representative.

Sell houses and other real property. An executor can sell a house, even over the heirs' objections—and in many cases, they do, either to pay estate expenses or to fairly distribute the estate among the beneficiaries.

EXAMPLE: Mrs. Velshi left her estate, which included the family home, to be divided equally among her four children. Helen, the youngest daughter, wanted to keep the home herself, but she was unable to secure financing to buy out the other siblings' shares. The executor had to sell the house in order to fairly distribute the estate, even though it was very painful for Helen to see it sold.

Sign checks and manage estate account. The executor opens an estate account and deposits all of the estate's assets into that account. He has full legal authority to write and sign checks on behalf of the estate.

Pay expenses and settle debts. The executor is responsible for the estate's expenses and debts once he is duly appointed. He must follow a specific order of payment, and if he makes a mistake—for example, if he pays a bill out of order or overlooks a debt—he has to cover the error out of his own pocket. Hidden debts often come to light after someone dies.

EXAMPLE: Donovan was the executor of his brother Wendell's estate. When Wendell's ex-wife of 12 years learned of his death, her lawyer contacted Donovan to collect on nearly $40,000 in unpaid alimony under her spousal support decree. She had been unwilling to press the issue while Wendell was alive, but felt she deserved to be paid out of the estate before his current wife inherited.

Evict tenants, even if they are beneficiaries. Evicting someone is a job no executor relishes, but it is sometimes necessary, even and perhaps *especially* when the tenant stands to inherit.

EXAMPLE: Alyson lived with her father in his home in New York for the last 10 years of his life. After his death, Alyson asked the executor—her brother Bryce, who lived in Seattle—if she could remain in the house a couple of months until she could find a new place to live. Bryce accommodated her for as long as he could, but he needed cash from the house to settle the estate's debts. He finally gave Alyson an ultimatum to vacate the house within two weeks, but she dragged her feet.

Bryce was forced to begin eviction procedures to remove his sister from the home so he could sell it.

File tax returns. The executor doesn't have to *prepare* the actual tax returns, but he is the only one with legal authority to sign and file them on behalf of the deceased and the estate.

The job gets even more complex if there is estate tax due. Although this is relatively uncommon for U.S. citizens, it's surprisingly *common* for foreign citizens holding U.S. assets —the estate tax cutoff for non-resident aliens is just $60,000.

EXAMPLE: Mr. Chen was a Chinese citizen living in China, but he owned a $500,000 condo as well as a U.S. brokerage account containing $100,000 for use by his two children attending college in California. After his death, his estate owed taxes on the value of his condo and investments in excess of $60,000.

Inform beneficiaries of progress on settlement. The executor must make reasonable efforts to keep beneficiaries in the loop during the settlement process. This doesn't mean consulting with them or asking permission before actions are taken, but it does mean giving occasional progress reports so the heirs know what to expect.

EXECUTORS VS. TRUSTEES

Don't confuse the executor with the trustee, if there is one. The executor's job is time-limited and transactional. Most estates are settled within three years, with the average falling in the range of 12 to 18 months.

A trustee, on the other hand, could be on the job for decades. It's potentially a long-term relationship.

EXAMPLE: When Mr. Brooks died, he left the bulk of his estate in trust for his three children, currently aged 21, 18, and 4, until they reach the age of 30. His lawyer, Mr. Thomas, was the estate executor, and his duties were finished in about a year. Ms. Rodriguez, the trustee, is responsible for managing the money in trust for the next 26 years, until the youngest child turns 30.

Some people ask if the executor and trustee can be the same person. There's no legal prohibition against naming the same person for both jobs. However, keep in mind that while an older person may reasonably be expected to carry out the duties of an executor, he may not be in a position—depending on his age—to serve as trustee for a period of 10 or 20 years or more.

PROFESSIONAL EXECUTORS: AN ANSWER TO A DIFFICULT PROBLEM

If you haven't guessed from reading this far, being an executor is a *lot* of work. It's not even the nature of the job that's so difficult—it's complying with all the local laws and financial rules and regulations that, in many cases, exhaust family members and friends pressed into the job. If you and the deceased live in the same general area, being the executor may be manageable. However, if you and the estate are in two different cities or countries, it can be very burdensome.

An executor's duties can't be scheduled for a few hours one Saturday a month—at times, it's an all-consuming task made even worse by structural issues in the legal and corporate system. For example:

1. **There's no delegating your authority as an executor.** You have to do every task yourself, which means spending hours on the phone with the bank or insurance company, or standing in line at the courthouse filing papers. If you live in the same area as the deceased, it's a hassle. If you have to fly in from another country or state just to close the deceased's checking account, it's an expensive nightmare.

2. **Probate technology hasn't caught up with the real world.** Take opening a bank account—in the real world, you can do it online or through an app. In the probate world, it requires a

trip to the bank with your court-certified letters testamentary in hand. And that's just the tip of the iceberg. Just about everything you're used to doing electronically has to be done with paper, in triplicate, usually after a long wait trying to find someone who knows how to handle a probate issue.

3. **You're caught in the middle.** On the asset side, you're dealing with banks, insurance companies, and government agencies known for dragging their feet. On the debit side, you have tax collectors, creditors, and heirs who want money or answers *right now*. It's not an enviable position.

4. **You don't get rich serving as an executor.** Executor fees are set by state law and typically a percentage of the estate. When you divide your pay by the number of hours involved—and deduct the travel expenses flying back and forth if you're not local to the estate—you could end up working for free.

5. **The risk is real.** You are financially responsible for actions you take on behalf of the estate. Make a mistake, even an honest one, and it could cost you. And it's a risk that doesn't end once the estate is settled. If there's not a formal judicial accounting, heirs can file a lawsuit years later over your actions. Legal representation isn't free and the estate doesn't pay your costs.

As we'll get into in later chapters, there is a solution to the pitfalls presented above. Those who aren't keen to take on the hassle of settling an estate—or don't wish to burden a family member or friend with the task—can hire a professional executor to handle the entire process for them.

EXAMPLE: Peter moved to London from his native Buffalo to pursue a career in international finance. His mother had been dead for several years, but he was unprepared when he got the call that his father had suddenly died of a heart attack.

After spending $2,500 for an unplanned flight to arrange his father's funeral and final affairs, Peter was surprised to learn that he was the named executor of his father's will. But given modern technology, he figured he could manage the tasks from his home in London with maybe one more trip back to New York to sign off on the sale of his father's home at some point in the future.

Things didn't turn out quite the way Peter expected. He was shocked to discover that he needed letters testamentary in order to handle his father's estate—and the process required another trip and extended stay in New York to obtain.

Then the real nightmare began. He was unable to open an estate account in New York without personally appearing at the bank—another $2,500 trip and week away from work. Simple things such as arranging to forward mail also required an in-person visit to the post office. In frustration, he tried to give power of attorney to his Aunt Theresa in Buffalo to handle some of the legwork, but learned his executor's authority could not be delegated.

All in all, he figured he would need to make at least 5 or 6 trips to New York over the next several months to handle the known issues involved in settling the estate, not to mention the unplanned and unexpected things that might come up during the process. The costs could easily exceed $10,000 in travel alone, not to mention the issues his absence created with his job.

Peter quickly concluded the only answer would be to hire a professional executor to handle his father's affairs. Even taking executor's fees into account, the decision actually saved Peter a significant amount of money—and an infinite amount of aggravation and frustration.

KEY TAKEAWAYS

- An executor has a great deal of power and

authority—and an equal amount of responsibility for tasks that only he *personally* can do.

- Most of an executor's tasks are done in the county where the estate is probated, requiring many in-person meetings and appearances at banks, courthouses, and government offices.
- An executor often has to make difficult decisions on behalf of the estate that upset or offend the heirs.
- An executor's job is made harder by a legal and corporate probate structure that doesn't operate using modern technology and protocols.

CHAPTER 2

WHO IS USUALLY THE EXECUTOR?

YOU MIGHT THINK something as personal as your choice of executor is outside the reach of the legal system, but you'd be wrong. States have laws regarding who can be confirmed as the executor of your estate.

Although the laws may vary a bit from state to state—and even county to county—generally speaking, the following requirements must be met before a court will approve an executor:

- The person must be a U.S. citizen at least 21 years of age (18 in some cases). Some states don't actually prohibit non-citizens from serving as executors, especially if the non-citizen executor is the surviving spouse. However, non-citizens usually can't get a probate bond, which the court may require.
- The executor must live in the same state or county as the deceased. Some states will allow an out-of-

state executor, but it's not an ideal situation given the sheer number of tasks that need to be completed in the deceased's home jurisdiction. Courts strongly prefer a local executor.

- There can be no felony convictions on the person's record. Again, some states will allow a named executor with a criminal record to be confirmed as long as he can be bonded. However, it's almost impossible for a convicted felon to get a probate bond, so even if it's technically allowed, it almost never actually happens in real life.

- The person must be financially responsible. The most common measure of financial responsibility is a credit score; a person with poor credit may not qualify for a bond if required by the court.

EXAMPLE: Mrs. Pham named her good friend and next door neighbor, Mr. Flynn, as her executor. The court in her jurisdiction required all executors to get an estate bond in order to serve. Unfortunately, Mr. Flynn's export business had failed a couple of years ago, and he was forced to file bankruptcy. The bonding company deemed Mr. Flynn a credit risk and wouldn't issue a bond, so he was unable to be confirmed as the executor even though he was named in the will.

Other states may have additional requirements for executor eligibility. North Carolina, for example, requires executors to be literate in English, Texas courts can exclude executors they consider "unsuitable," and Florida requires executors to be related to the deceased person. In all states, the court generally has the final authority over who can be duly appointed as executor, regardless of the provisions in the will.

WHAT USUALLY HAPPENS WHEN A LONG-DISTANCE RELATIVE DIES

When a family member dies in a distant state or country, the surviving relatives are often in a bind. They know they need a local representative to settle their loved one's affairs, but they usually don't know anyone near the deceased's home.

Most family members look to their loved one's neighbors or friends to serve as the executor. Failing that, they look for *any* connection, no matter how distant, living in the deceased's country or local jurisdiction.

This is a recipe for disaster on multiple levels. Neighbors and casual friends typically don't want to commit a year or more of their lives to settling an acquaintance's final affairs —and many lack the time, knowledge, and credit history to be approved.

EXAMPLE: Mary met her husband, James, when he was stationed in the Philippines, and she left her family in Manila to move with him to California. Their only daughter died in childhood, and after James died, Mary considered returning to her family in Manila, but in the end, she stayed in San Diego.

When Mary passed away, her family in the Philippines realized they would need someone in San Diego to settle her affairs, but unfortunately they didn't know anyone there.

Mary's nephew John Mark had completed a semester abroad in Arizona some 20 years ago and still kept in touch with his host family, the Dixons, in Glendale. He contacted them to see if someone would be willing to handle Mary's estate. Mrs. Dixon reluctantly agreed, but John Mark came to regret the decision.

Mrs. Dixon was out of her depth with all of the court filings and financial records, as well as managing the sale of Mary's home, which fetched far less than market value due to Mrs. Dixon's impatience and inexperience. Mary's family felt things were being handled poorly, if at all, yet they couldn't really complain because they knew Mrs. Dixon was doing them a favor. Nearly 30 months later, the estate still hadn't been settled.

WHAT USUALLY HAPPENS WHEN A PERSON WRITES A WILL

Your family lawyer is an obvious choice for executor, but a lot of people overlook the obvious and go another route. Quite often, they approach choosing an executor in the same way they would choose a best man or maid of honor from among their pool of friends.

There is some merit in choosing your best friend to serve as an executor. She's likely someone you trust with the most important details in your life, and she would probably look out for your best interests.

But there are two major flaws with the best-friend-as-executor approach:

- Someone so close to you needs time to grieve and mourn the loss of her best friend. It's probably not the right time to ask her to commit to a year or more of digging into your financial affairs and dealing with the family pain and drama death often brings.
- Your best friend may not be qualified to serve, or have enough time to manage the tasks involved in settling your estate.

EXAMPLE: When Cecile was diagnosed with end-stage pancreatic cancer, she asked her dearest friend, Marta, an estate attorney, to serve as her executor. It seemed like the perfect choice, and Marta was happy to accept. However, when Cecile died four months later, it didn't seem like such a good decision.

Although Marta knew exactly what needed to be done, she was distracted by grief and forgot the most basic things. When Cecile's sisters in Quebec, who had stayed away for the worst part of Cecile's illness, called Marta for perfectly normal reasons, she struggled to be polite because she resented their lack of involvement in Cecile's life. What should have been just another case in Marta's busy law practice became a miserable task and a painful reminder of her best friend's tragic death.

Another common approach is to name the most responsible family member, which is often the eldest child. This isn't necessarily a bad decision, but it comes with a huge burden of responsibility at a time of devastating loss.

EXAMPLE: Laila and her mother had always been exceptionally close. As the firstborn, Laila was her mother's constant companion and helper as she struggled to learn English from her native Urdu and understand the new customs and culture in America. Laila kept house and looked after her four younger brothers. Mrs. Emani could always rely on her, even after Laila married, left the home, and had children of her own.

It was no surprise that Laila was named the executor of her mother's will. Her father had suffered a stroke several years ago and was partially paralyzed. Her brothers had scattered across the country with their families. Although it was expected, Laila found herself angry at the added responsibility. Not only was she caring for her ailing father, she had two young children of her own and a husband with a fledgling medical practice that consumed his time. All she wanted was time to grieve her mother and adjust to her new reality.

Instead, Laila faced two years of sorting out her mother's finances, making arrangements for her father's care, and dealing with the petty grievances of her brothers, who would no doubt disapprove of the decisions she made.

WHEN SOMEONE DIES INTESTATE

More people die *without* a will (intestate) than die *with* one —currently, about 60% of the population dies intestate.

State intestacy laws kick in when someone dies without a valid will. The court follows a set of established procedures to name an executor based on next of kin. First in line is a surviving spouse, followed by children, siblings, and other extended family members.

Should the spouse be the executor of a will?

In many cases, the surviving spouse is a natural fit for executor. Most couples today are financial partners, and each knows the important details about the family's income, assets, and expenses.

Potential problems crop up in the case of blended families, when the surviving spouse is not the biological parent of the deceased's children, or there is an ex-wife or ex-husband in the picture who shares custody of the biological kids.

And again, in a time of deep mourning, it may be asking too much of the surviving spouse to settle the final affairs.

EXAMPLE: Arielle was Ivan's second wife and the mother of his two-year-old son. Ivan shared custody of his 17-year-old twin daughters with his ex-wife, Nadia. When Ivan died suddenly without a valid will, the court appointed Arielle as the executor of his estate.

Arielle was devastated by Ivan's death and could barely get through the funeral arrangements, let alone face the task of dealing with Ivan's complicated finances. To make matters worse, Nadia had never accepted her divorce and Ivan's marriage to Arielle, and she was resentful of the couple's son. She felt sure, with Arielle in charge of the money, that her daughters would be short-changed on their inheritance and the promise Ivan had made to pay for the girls' college educations would be ignored.

Arielle was on the verge of emotional collapse from the stress of Ivan's death and Nadia's constant harassment. She ultimately declined the job and asked the court to appoint someone else to settle the estate.

Other family members as executors

There's always an *appearance* of conflict when a family member, who is also a beneficiary, serves as the executor. If the executor is one of the deceased's children, the others perceive an imbalance of power—which, of course, there is. Remember, the executor has the final say on most decisions involved in settling the estate.

The same situation occurs when the executor is one of a group of siblings or other family members who also stand to inherit from the estate. Even if the executor's actions are unimpeachably correct, other heirs may still question them or find fault.

EXAMPLE: Winston and his brother, Lloyd, emigrated from Jamaica to New York together as young men. When Winston passed away, his will named Lloyd as executor.

Winston had done well for himself financially, and in addition to his assets in New York, he had bought homes in Jamaica for his two sisters, which were titled in his name. Winston and his late wife had no children—his will left his estate to be divided equally among his three surviving siblings.

Lloyd's executorship got off to a rocky start because the Jamaica sisters insisted that their homes be transferred to their names immediately. They felt Lloyd was dragging his feet and keeping them in the dark about Winston's estate.

For his part, Lloyd was overwhelmed by the legal processes involved in settling an estate with foreign property, not to mention the competing tax laws and paperwork. At every turn, his sisters accused him of acting in his own interests at the expense of theirs. At nearly 70 years old, Lloyd was not a young man, and he found the situation bewildering and exhausting. He regretted ever accepting the job, and ultimately turned the estate over to a professional executor to untangle.

KEY TAKEAWAYS

- Even executors named in a will must meet certain minimum legal requirements to be certified by the court.
- When the deceased and his heirs live in different countries, the heirs may be unable to find a qualified local executor from their personal connections or their loved one's local social circle.
- Although it seems sensible to have a surviving spouse or family member serve as executor, an executor who is also an heir often creates a new set of problems.
- Don't underestimate the emotional toll of the death of a loved one or close friend—someone who is grieving your loss may not be the best choice for executor.

CHAPTER 3

WHAT HAPPENS WHEN YOU HAVE A SUBOPTIMAL EXECUTOR

WHAT MAKES AN EXECUTOR SUBOPTIMAL? Any of a number of things can do it—a lack of time for, or interest in, doing the job, an inability to make wise and timely decisions, inattention to detail, and poor record-keeping skills are a few good examples.

Distance, however, is perhaps the biggest handicap for an executor. Long-distance executors usually lack familiarity with local laws, connections to local resources, and understanding of common customs and processes for liquidating assets and settling an estate.

If you've chosen a suboptimal executor, you'll know soon enough. Here are a few possibilities you might face:

THE EXECUTOR WON'T START THE JOB

There are things an executor must do to get the probate process started: Apply for letters testamentary, file a petition for probate with the court, notify beneficiaries, obtain a tax ID number for the estate, open an estate bank account... you get the idea.

It's normal human nature, when faced with a series of complex and time-consuming tasks related to a subject you know nothing about, to find reasons to avoid doing them.

EXAMPLE: Lena was pregnant with her fourth child when her father died at his assisted living center in Arizona and she learned she was the executor. She and her husband had recently moved to Chicago and she was trying to unpack and settle into their new home, get her older kids enrolled in school, and keep on top of their realtor to sell the house in Sacramento they had just left.

When Lena returned to Chicago after the funeral, she spent her rare moments of free time the first week researching what she had to do to get started. She soon realized she would need a lawyer in Phoenix to help her get letters testamentary, so she spent the next two weeks Googling potential candidates and playing phone tag to arrange a conversation. Lena finally found one she was comfortable with only to learn his practice was in Maricopa County and her father's estate would be probated in Pinal County, so she had to start her search over from scratch.

At every step, Lena's lack of familiarity both with estate law and Arizona geography impeded her progress, and she was constantly retracing her steps because of it. Nothing was straightforward; every task required layers and layers of research and endless phone calls. The process was so frustrating, she began to look for any excuse to avoid working on the estate. When her brother called from Geneva some months later asking for a progress report, she exploded. Despite spending hundreds of hours chasing information, Lena was no closer to settling the estate that when she started.

THE EXECUTOR REFUSES THE JOB

A person isn't obligated to serve just because you name him in your will—and when the executor doesn't want the job, he can't be legally compelled.

When you write your will, it's important to have a conversation with the person you choose as your executor to make sure he is willing to serve. It's a conversation you should revisit every few years, because circumstances change, and someone who was happy to accept the job five or ten years ago may feel differently now.

EXAMPLE: Rafi's accountant and best friend, Gilad, was honored when Rafi asked him to be his executor twenty-five years ago, and Gilad gladly accepted. So Rafi's lawyer drafted his will naming Gilad as executor, and Rafi filed the document away, considering the issue settled. Three decades later, Gilad retired and moved from New York to Tel Aviv.

When Itra, Rafi's widow, called Gilad to tell him Rafi died, he was surprised to learn Rafi hadn't changed his will in the intervening years. He declined the executor appointment: he hadn't practiced in the U.S. in years and had no active contacts in the States. As much as he cared for his friend, he knew he was in no position to settle Rafi's financial affairs long-distance.

THE EXECUTOR IS OVERWHELMED

Unlike the executor who won't get started, the overwhelmed executor files the correct paperwork and gets things underway before realizing she's completely out of her depth. She agonizes over every decision, ultimately refusing to make one because she's paralyzed by a fear of personal risk.

Often, the overwhelmed executor lives overseas or out of the deceased's jurisdiction. She's unfamiliar with local laws, and may not feel comfortable hiring a broker to sell her mother's house long-distance, for example. The probate process grinds to a halt, and the heirs are in the dark about what's happening.

Even when she knows what steps she should take, the overwhelmed executor hesitates out of fear she's making a mistake. If that sounds like your executor, it could be years before the estate is settled and the money is distributed.

EXAMPLE: After Marine's father died, she assumed her 62-year-old mother would continue on indefinitely with her life in Paris. She was surprised when her mother met an American banker, fell madly in love, and moved to New York with him. She was shocked when her mother died just two years later, leaving her affairs in Marine's hands.

At first, Marine felt competent to manage her mother's estate. She was able to arrange to have her mother's body returned to France for her funeral, but things went downhill quickly after that. The rules regarding her mother's co-op were incomprehensible, and she had no idea how the American private health insurance system worked when it came to settling her mother's medical bills.

To make matter worse, the time difference made it very difficult to reach local officials to get answers to her questions.

Marine's sisters were exasperated with her lack of progress, and Marine felt frozen in place. She considered herself bilingual in English and French, but her vocabulary didn't include the words she needed to deal with the American probate system. A year after her mother's death, she was no closer to settling her estate than she was the day she died. She realized she needed an American executor to handle her mother's affairs.

THE EXECUTOR IS DISHONEST

This is extraordinarily rare, but it must be mentioned. Sometimes a person pressed into acting as executor behaves unethically and intentionally defrauds the estate.

Families are most vulnerable to a dishonest executor when they reach out to a neighbor or acquaintance whom they've never met simply because this person is the only one they "know" who lived near their loved one. Outright stealing from the estate is less common, but there are other ways a dishonest executor takes advantage of the heirs.

Pro tip: If your executor is strangely averse to providing an accounting, or flat-out refuses to show his work, you should probably worry—and insist on a formal accounting.

EXAMPLE: Mrs. Liu's neighbor Mr. Brown took it upon himself to notify her family in China that she had passed away. Weeks later, the Lius asked Mr. Brown to be the executor for their sister, because he was the only person they knew in the U.S. who could help them. Mr. Brown reluctantly agreed.

When Mr. Brown cleaned out Mrs. Liu's condo, he discovered nearly $5,000 in cash strategically hidden in her belongings. It crossed his mind to deposit the money in the estate account, but his daughter had asked him for help with buying a house, and Mrs. Liu's $5,000 would come in very handy. So he pocketed the money to give to his daughter and didn't record it as part of the estate.

Two months later, Mr. Brown had a medical emergency that strained his budget. The realtor had recommended a new paint job and a few minor repairs before he listed Mrs. Liu's condo for sale, so Mr. Brown hired a friend to complete the work and billed the estate twice the amount his friend charged. He used the extra money to pay his medical bills.

Over the next year, he discovered other clever ways to pad his expenses and line his pocket. In the end, Mrs. Liu's family lost over $12,000 to Mr. Brown's schemes, but they had no way of knowing it.

REMOVING AN EXECUTOR

Sometimes, removal is the only option for dealing with a suboptimal executor. It is legally possible to remove an executor, but the process is slow and expensive.

The first step is to petition the court. The heirs must demonstrate to the court that the appointed executor is unfit to serve. There are hearings, and the process moves at the same glacial pace as you'd expect from probate court. Removal doesn't happen overnight, or even within a month or two.

The new executor goes through the same appointment process as the original one. It can take six weeks or more to be duly appointed and obtain the proper legal documents. To make matters worse, the court may require an accounting from the first executor before the new executor takes over the job.

A judicial accounting is a cumbersome process in which every transaction is reviewed and every dollar is accounted for so the new executor starts with a clean slate. It's both time-consuming and expensive, but in the case of a truly inadequate or dishonest executor, it's necessary—and may even save the estate money in the long term.

The same applies when an executor quits after being confirmed. No matter how the executor is removed, forcibly or voluntarily, the replacement process is the same.

EXAMPLE: Luca's father moved from Milan to Washington, D.C., for what was supposed to be a three-year post with his job. He died unexpectedly at his home in Virginia, and Luca was the executor of his estate. Although Luca was not certain he was up to the task of managing his father's affairs from Italy, he thought at worst he'd realize he was in over his head and just hire a professional executor to finish the job.

Six months later, that's precisely what happened: Luca was in over his head, and he knew the job was too complex to handle from 4,000 miles away. He thought it would be fairly straightforward to "resign" his executorship and hire a pro. Unfortunately, the process took over four months to complete and cost the estate thousands of dollars.

Obviously, it's best to avoid a suboptimal executor altogether and choose well the first time. Whether that means taking precautions when you write your will, or hiring a professional executor when the named executor is unable or unfit to serve, everyone is better off when the appointed executor is able and willing to do the job.

KEY TAKEAWAYS

- An otherwise qualified executor is a bad choice

when family circumstances or distance prevents him from doing his job correctly.

- It's difficult, but not impossible, for an executor to steal from an estate, especially when the deceased's family is long-distance.
- It is possible to remove an executor, but it's costly and time-consuming. You're much better off spending the time and money to get it right the first time.

CHAPTER 4

WHAT IS A PROFESSIONAL EXECUTOR?

MANY, if not most of us, outsource some of our tasks to professionals. It helps us get things done when we lack the time or expertise to do them ourselves. You might not think twice about paying someone to do your taxes, sell your home, walk your dog, plan your wedding, or even care for your aging relatives. But what about settling an estate?

While the idea of hiring a professional to settle a loved one's final affairs isn't as common as it should be, considering what's required of an executor, it's getting there. As families and heirs become more aware of their options, more of them are opting to hire a professional executor.

WHO CAN BE A PROFESSIONAL EXECUTOR?

Professional executors are either licensed individuals (usually lawyers—although some states recognize non-lawyer professional executors), or regulated corporations such as banks and trust corporations.

The average Joe can't launch a Facebook page, print up business cards, and advertise his services online as a professional executor. It's not nearly as simple as opening a dog-walking business, for example, or even a tax preparation service.

Professional executors must be bonded and insured—which makes sense, because they are legally responsible for handling other people's money, i.e., estate assets. Lawyers carry malpractice policies with separate riders to cover them when they act as professional executors. Even with malpractice coverage, some courts require an executor bond.

The situation is a bit different with a bank or trust department. These institutions are already heavily regulated at both the federal and state level and subject to capital and liquidity requirements. In other words, financial corporations have ample cash in reserve, so they are essentially self-insured.

ADVANTAGES OF A PROFESSIONAL EXECUTOR

For most people, the convenience factor and the assurance that things will be handled as quickly and competently as possible tilt the scales in favor of hiring a professional.

Professional executors handle hundreds of estates. What you find baffling and exhausting is all in a day's work for them. They have the local resources and contacts to handle everything from cleaning out a loved one's apartment to arranging the sale of business equipment.

Professional executors are staffed out to quickly and efficiently accomplish routine tasks and resolve unexpected problems. They have relationships at probate court, connections with the estate departments at local banks, a rolodex of real estate brokers and investors, and paralegals to complete paperwork and deal with the IRS call center.

Impartiality, however, may be the most persuasive argument for hiring a pro. A professional executor represents the estate—not you or any other beneficiaries or heirs. He is legally obligated to be transparent, objective, and diligent while carrying out your loved one's wishes (or the laws of the state in the absence of a valid will). Everyone is treated fairly.

EXAMPLE: Isobel decided to hire Mr. Bertram, a professional executor, to settle her father's estate in New York. Isobel was a cruise director for a major cruise line—her home base in Miami and extended periods at sea made it difficult to deal with the probate process in New York.

Within the first three months of being duly appointed, Mr. Bertram had initiated probate, notified heirs, opened a bank account, sold off her father's stocks and bonds, arranged to have his condo cleaned, repaired, and listed for sale, and compiled a list of debts and expenses. Isobel and her brothers knew all of this because Mr. Bertram e-mailed them regularly to keep them in the loop on what he'd accomplished so far, upcoming tasks, and the timeline to settlement.

Even Isobel's cranky older brother, Thomas, found nothing to complain about, and he had been critical of their father's decision to name Isobel as executor in his will. All three siblings felt confident Mr. Bertram had things well in hand and would honor their father's wishes.

ATTORNEY VS. BANK AS PROFESSIONAL EXECUTOR

Since you can choose either a lawyer or a bank to handle your estate, it's important to understand the advantages and disadvantages of each.

Lawyers are more accessible—by virtue of their lower estate minimums. Most lawyers set their minimum estate value at $250,000 to $500,000 before they accept a case (and some have no minimums at all).

Banks, on the other hand, generally won't touch estates with less than $1 million in *investable* assets: houses, cars, and life insurance policies don't count toward the total.

Some banks set the threshold much higher—$2 million or even $5 million isn't uncommon, and you may even need the trust department's approval before the bank takes your case. Unless you're dealing with a *very* large estate, you likely won't be able to hire a bank.

Advantages of hiring a lawyer

- **A lawyer has "skin in the game."** There is significant exposure to personal financial liability and risk for attorneys acting as professional executors. But beyond that, their livelihood and professional reputation is also on the line when they take your case. A lawyer who mishandles an estate could lose his standing at the probate courts he regularly appears in—and even his law license.

- **A lawyer usually knows estate, probate, and tax law.** In other words, it's a very efficient relationship because a lawyer has the expertise to navigate the legal issues covering every aspect of the estate.

- **A lawyer-executor can act independently.** Although the lawyer-executor may be qualified to handle the legal and tax work on the estate, he also has the authority to hire outside counsel when it would best serve the interests of the estate.

EXAMPLE: Ms. Javitt was the professional executor for the Herrera estate. Although she had tax law expertise within her own firm, she opted to hire a law firm specializing in estate tax law to manage the complicated tax issues involved in settling the estate. This, she felt, offered more control and transparency over expenses, and by hiring a firm experienced with the specific tax issues in the Herrera estate, she knew the billable hours would likely be lower than if she used her own associate, who was a tax law generalist, for the work.

- **A lawyer can assume other roles for estate planning purposes.** You can give your lawyer power of attorney to make financial decisions for you if you are incapacitated, or appoint him as your health care proxy to make medical decisions on your behalf.

It's important to point out that a professional executor is *not* your personal lawyer; his duty lies only to the estate. It's a significant distinction.

EXAMPLE: The Kapoors, who lived in Delhi, hired Mr. Pierce as the professional executor for their son Arjun's estate. Arjun had died unexpectedly while completing his medical training in New York. As he had no will, state law designated Mr. and Mrs. Kapoor as Arjun's heirs.

Some weeks into the probate process, however, a young woman announced that her child was Arjun's biological son, even though they had never married. The Kapoors were surprised that Mr. Pierce wouldn't take their side in this matter. But Mr. Pierce, as executor, was obligated to act on behalf of Arjun's estate, and if paternity tests established Arjun as the boy's father, the boy would indeed be the sole legal heir absent a will. At first, the Kapoors were not pleased they had to hire a separate attorney to handle the conflict, but they ultimately understood.

Finally, lawyers are people, too, which means they get sick, take vacation, and yes, even die, which may complicate the settlement process.

Advantages of hiring a bank

If your loved one's estate is large enough to get past the trust department's threshold, there are a few advantages to choosing a bank as your executor.

- **Banks, like other corporate entities, are "immortal."** Banks, unlike individuals, don't die. The bank will always be there, in one form or another, regardless of the individual officers working on your case.
- **Banks may have expertise on complex or esoteric assets.** Banks handling large estates often have in-house staff able to appraise an art or jewelry collection, or unravel an unusual financial arrangement or business asset.

There are definite drawbacks, however, to going the bank route. For example, trust officers may not be attorneys familiar with the nuances of probate and tax law, which may make them less efficient than a lawyer.

EXAMPLE: Because of their long-standing trust relationship with a local bank, the Wentworth family chose it to act as executor of their father's sprawling estate. Because the heirs and beneficiaries were scattered across several states and countries, there were several questions regarding the various tax issues involved.

However, Ms. Sutton, the trust officer assigned to their case, was a banker and did not have a tax or legal background. Each time she fielded a call or question from a family member, several days would elapse before she was able to consult a lawyer and supply the answer.

And if you're in the estate planning phase and thinking of naming a bank as executor, there are definite limitations. For example, you can't give a bank power of attorney or name it your health care proxy.

Banks merge, get acquired, or overhaul their image and culture *all the time.* If you have a long-standing relationship with your local branch of Federal United Bank, and you choose them as executor because you appreciate their conservative approach, you might be in for a rude surprise when they are acquired by Digital Now Bank.

The quiet, comfortable branch with helpful tellers and the manager seated behind a mahogany desk is replaced by something that looks more like a hipster coffee shop than a bank. And there's no such thing as a teller anymore because banking is done via smartphone app.

It happens, and for some people, it's no big deal. For others? It's a major deal-breaker.

But the most important thing to keep in mind if you're choosing a bank is that banks, by definition, have a conflict of interest. There's a strong incentive to keep your money tied up in the bank's interconnected products and services.

The old checking-and-savings bank model has been replaced by financial conglomerates offering everything from insurance products to IRAs and mutual funds. Even if your money might be better off in another investment long-term, banks will subtly (or not so subtly) make the case for leaving your money with them because it's better for the bank's bottom line.

Finally, banks are also staffed by human beings...and just as with lawyers, your bank trust officer might get sick, take vacation, find a new job, etc. Although there's *institutional* continuity with a bank, there's no guarantee of *personal* continuity.

KEY TAKEAWAYS

- Although both lawyers and banks can act as professional executors, banks generally only deal with estates of $1 million or more, not including real estate and life insurance.
- Lawyer-executors have the advantage of offering one-stop-shopping for estate planning, probate law, and tax expertise.
- If you're writing your will, keep in mind that lawyers, not banks, can have power of attorney over your financial decisions and act as your health care proxy to make medical decisions on your behalf.

CHAPTER 5

WHY APPOINT A PROFESSIONAL EXECUTOR?

HERE'S a fact that might surprise you: executor fees are set either by state law or by the terms of the will—and they are the same no matter who does the job.

In other words, whether your crazy Uncle Clyde serves as executor or you hire a professional to handle your affairs, *the estate pays the exact same amount.*

Let that sink in for a minute.

The Zeldins, who lived on the East Coast, were at a loss to find a local executor when Melba, Mr. Zeldin's spinster aunt, died thousands of miles away in Idaho. When it was discovered that Rufus, Mr. Zeldin's cousin twice removed, lived a few minutes away from Melba's hometown, they believed they had found the perfect solution. After all, he was still family, and that was better than a stranger, they reasoned.

Rufus was an unemployed musician, so even though he had no idea what was required of him, he had plenty of spare time and he figured he could use the money. He was happy to accept the job.

His enthusiasm disappeared when he learned he would not get paid upfront. Rufus took several months to get formally appointed and open probate. During that time, the tenant living in the basement of Aunt Melba's house had paid no rent, and knowing a good situation when she saw one, had no intention of paying now—or moving out, for that matter, just because Rufus finally got around to asking her to. As long as she paid the utility bills each month, she didn't see any reason the arrangement shouldn't continue indefinitely.

Rufus was a non-confrontational guy and couldn't bring himself to evict her, or do much else, quite frankly, to settle the estate. He had recently started a band and now spent most of his time rehearsing for his wedding reception gigs.

Meanwhile, the county served notice on the estate that Melba's house would be sold at auction if the past-due property taxes weren't paid. The tax bill had slipped Rufus's mind.

Rufus, realizing he was in over his head, finally hired a lawyer, who charged the estate several thousand dollars to handle the situation with the county tax office, evict the entrenched tenant, and attempt to collect back rent. Realizing there was money to be made, the lawyer offered to "help" Rufus with other estate jobs, such as finding a realtor for Melba's house and listing her car on Craigslist and Facebook. These simple tasks that Rufus was too lazy or distracted to handle didn't require a lawyer, yet the estate was billed the hourly rate for legal work.

After nearly three years, countless delays and bungled decisions, Melba's estate was finally settled, although most of her assets had disappeared due to mismanagement and legal fees. The Zeldins knew they had a solid case against Rufus, but they were just relieved, at that point, to have the whole ordeal over. Mr. Zeldin was glad that his aunt wasn't alive to see how Rufus had frittered away the money she had worked so hard to save over the years. He realized too late that he could have paid a professional executor the same amount the shiftless Rufus was given, and preserved so much more of poor Melba's money for her heirs.

WHEN HIRING A PROFESSIONAL EXECUTOR MAKES SENSE

If you're not sure if outsourcing the job to a professional executor is the right choice for you, there are several advantages to keep in mind.

A professional executor is local to the estate

Settling an estate is difficult for an out-of-state executor. For an out-of-the-country one, it becomes nearly impossible, but you know that from reading this book.

Aside from the convenience factor, however, the financial advantages to having a local professional executor are not insignificant. In addition to executor fees established by law, the executor can bill the estate for reasonable expenses.

EXAMPLE: When Mr. Herrera died in Texas, his family in Mexico asked Nicolas, a relative in Arizona, to settle his estate. Nicolas knew nothing about being an executor, so his first order of business was finding an attorney in Mr. Herrera's home town to advise him, an expense ultimately billed to the estate. His lawyer explained executor duties and the importance of keeping detailed records, including any expenses he incurred carrying out his job. Nicolas pointed out that traveling back and forth between Arizona and Texas was expensive; the lawyer told him the estate would reimburse him.

Nicolas did an admirable job handling Mr. Herrera's affairs, but when the final accounting was reviewed, the estate had spent several thousand dollars on legal advice, and thousands more on mileage, meals, and hotels for the many trips Nicolas made there to settle the estate. Mr. Herrera's heirs lost out on almost $10,000 they might otherwise have kept if they had hired a local lawyer-executor.

A professional executor is independent and unconflicted

When you hire a professional executor, he is focused on preserving the estate's assets and settling the deceased's final affairs in accordance with his wishes and state law.

In other words, he is not emotionally connected to the situation; he is impartial. He doesn't have a favorite child, he's not sentimental about Dad's old convertible, and cleaning out Grandma's attic isn't going to make him weep over childhood memories.

You can't say the same for family members or close personal friends.

EXAMPLE: Mrs. Rao's passion was breeding beautiful French bulldogs. The puppies from Duchess and Dozer, her championship pair, were in heavy demand across the country. When she died unexpectedly, the two dogs were still in their prime and worth several thousand dollars each as breeding stock.

Her son Nathan, the executor, proposed to sell the dogs. They were part of his mother's estate, after all, and it looked as if the money might be needed by the time all the debts and expenses were paid. But Martha, his sister, was horrified that Nathan could even consider selling her mother's pride and joy.

The dogs became a source of heated arguments. Nathan agreed to house them temporarily, but they chewed his furniture and soiled his rugs. Martha refused to take them, saying her son was allergic. Yet she remained adamant that the dogs should not be sold.

Finally, Nathan reached his limit and found a buyer for the dogs, generating $18,000 for the estate. Martha was furious. The "Dog Day Massacre," as she melodramatically referred to the sale, launched a bitter feud that ruined their relationship for many years.

Keep in mind, however, that while hiring a professional can

often *avert* a family feud, it can rarely solve an existing one. If your family is already deeply conflicted over the will and threatening to sue over this provision or that, you'll be hard pressed to find an executor to take your case. He can see the writing on the wall, and given the personal risk involved in the job, he'll politely refuse.

Professional executors are insured and bonded

Outright theft, especially with family members, is rare, but incompetence is not. The good thing about hiring a professional is that heirs and beneficiaries are protected if he makes a mistake.

If mismanagement, intentional or not, costs the estate, the judge may order the executor to cover the damages. His malpractice insurance and/or bond are your guarantee he will pay it.

Unless the court requires a bond, you have to trust your friend or family member executor will do a good job. If he doesn't, even if you get a judge's order for damages, there's no assurance she has the money to reimburse the estate.

EXAMPLE: Meena was pressed into serving as executor of her neighbor Mr. Nguyen's estate by his family in Vietnam. She didn't know much about him, except that he earned his living fishing off the Florida coast. She'd been on his boat once and thought it was pretty.

Meena emptied his apartment, sold his furniture at a yard sale, and set about selling his old Honda sedan and his fishing boat. Meena knew nothing about boats, but after an hour or two on Google, based on pictures of boats she thought were similar to Mr. Nguyen's, she listed it for $5,000. Buyers began calling almost immediately and Meena was pleased when she got the full asking price.

Unfortunately, Mr. Nguyen's family members were not so pleased when they discovered the boat was actually worth more than $50,000, but there was really nothing they could do. Even if they had wanted to hire a lawyer to sue her, Meena had no assets or resources to repay the estate for her mistake.

Professional executors are...there

Some people choose not to marry and raise a family. Others leave their families behind to seek their fortunes in a new state or country. However you get there, the result is the same: sometimes people die with no relatives close by.

Professional executors are there when no one else is. Sure, you could spend a few weeks looking for a neighbor or acquaintance to do the job, but it's so much easier to do an online search for a local executor—and know that the job will be done right.

Professional executors relieve the burden on family members and friends

Even if you do have local family members or friends, they may not appreciate being asked to serve as executor. If you've read this book, you know it's a difficult, time-consuming, and often frustrating job. It's a big ask, even for someone who loves you.

If you're a family member from another state or country looking for a local acquaintance or contact to press into service—you're asking them to assume a huge (and likely unwelcome) burden.

Professional executors are there for just that purpose, to relieve the burden of settling an estate. They have the staff and expertise to do it quickly, efficiently, and as painlessly as possible for the heirs. Friends and family members can mourn and grieve and get on with their lives, leaving the business side of death to a professional.

KEY TAKEAWAYS

- Executor fees are the same whether you hire an inexperienced family member or a professional executor.
- Professional executors carry insurance that protects the heirs against theft, mismanagement, and financial loss.
- Professional executors make the hard but necessary decisions family members often can't.

CHAPTER 6

HOW TO HIRE A
PROFESSIONAL EXECUTOR

BY THIS POINT, you've probably realized that hiring a professional executor is the sensible way to go for most families. If you're an heir, there's really no downside—unless you like the idea of leaving your loved one's money in the hands of weird Uncle Joe, or worse yet, an unknown neighbor.

So the next question is how to go about hiring a professional executor.

HOW TO CHOOSE A PROFESSIONAL EXECUTOR

Now that you've made the decision to work with a professional, your next decision is to find the right one for your situation.

State law sets executor fees, which is great for heirs: you don't have to price-shop, so you can "shop" for an executor based on the things that really matter, such as experience and expert knowledge about the issues involved in your loved one's estate.

Right state

Most executors work in a specific state or geographic area. If your loved one's estate is in New York, you should choose an executor based in New York. Some executors do take estates outside their local jurisdiction, but don't assume that's the case. Make sure the executor you hire has experience in the city or county where the estate is located.

Professional experience

When it comes to executors, experience really does matter. You might find a will or estate planning attorney you like, but he's never *settled* an estate. There's a *huge* difference between drafting a will and settling an estate—and the learning curve is steep.

Make sure you ask how many cases your lawyer has handled as a professional executor—and think twice about hiring someone with fewer than 20 or 30 cases under his belt.

It's true you don't become an expert at something unless you do it several times, and sometimes it's nice to give the new guy a chance—but do you really want your loved one's estate to be a learning experience for your executor?

Skill stack

Think of the professional executor as the CEO of your estate. A good CEO should have a stack of high-level skills in many areas relating to his business. He doesn't need to know every line of the corporate and securities regulations, but he does need to know enough to ask the right questions to establish the right policies to guide the company and keep it in compliance.

Similarly, a good executor should have a skill stack that helps him understand all the estate's legal and financial issues and how to spot hidden problems. For example, tax law is a big part of settling an estate—especially if estate taxes come into play, which is almost always the case for foreign citizens with U.S. assets. Most executors (professional or otherwise) hire a CPA for tax preparation, but a good executor won't just blindly trust the accountant—he should have his own understanding of tax law, and be able identify potential tax issues and review the prepared returns before the IRS sees them.

Taxes are just one of the areas of concern in estate settlement, but settling your loved one's estate could require many other skills you should keep in mind before choosing an executor:

- **Real estate.** Selling a co-op in New York is *extremely* different from selling a residential property in Chicago or an investment property in Los Angeles. If there's real property in your loved one's estate, make sure your professional executor has experience with local real estate issues.
- **Business.** If your loved one owned a business or

had a partnership interest in one, there are a lot of issues the executor needs to unwind. Ask the executor about his experience unwinding different types of businesses or conducting the orderly transfer of businesses from one generation to the next.

- **Art.** Conserving the value of a loved one's art collection isn't something to leave in the hands of an inexperienced executor. If there is art in the estate, choose an executor with relationships and experience in the art world so the heirs get full value for your loved one's art collection.

- **Collectibles.** You might look at Grandpa's gun collection or Uncle William's comic books as simply a waste of space, but a good executor knows how to value (and liquidate) your loved one's collections.

- **Royalties.** Was your loved one an author? A composer? A musician? A photographer? You'd be surprised at the income stream generated by royalties. If that's part of the estate, choose an executor who knows how to get royalty payments assigned to the heirs.

Team or solo practice

Find out if your executor is a solo attorney or if there's a fully staffed office with a *team of legal professionals* supporting him. There's nothing technically *wrong* with a solo operation, but if you're dealing with a team, there's more efficient time management and continuity. A team can multitask in a way a lawyer operating independently cannot. When you consider all the tasks an executor has to complete to settle an estate, the team approach makes a world of difference.

Account minimums

Ask if your executor has an estate minimum. Most professional executors won't handle estates worth less than $250,000—and many set their minimums at $500,000 or more. The good news is that, unlike banks with their seven-figure minimums, most professional executors count real estate toward the estate minimum. Don't assume that's the case, however—be sure to ask.

A word about professional executors and international estates

Settling an estate is complicated enough when only one set of laws and institutional regulations come into play. But when you're dealing with the laws, customs, and financial institutions of two or more countries, the obstacles are multiplied.

It's not just the tax issues, although those are complex enough—it's understanding international banking systems, tax treaties, and how lawyers in other countries work.

If you're dealing with a multinational estate, don't scrimp on experience and expertise. Find a professional executor who knows how to handle the maze of connected issues with international estates.

WHEN A LOVED ONE DIES, FIRST THINGS FIRST

Heirs have two major decisions when a loved one dies—who will handle the funeral arrangements and who will handle the estate. In some cases, the same person takes care of both, especially if you live overseas from the deceased.

Remember, a professional executor is legally able to take charge of your loved one's remains and carry out the deceased's instructions (or the family's wishes, in the absence of a will). This is actually a *huge* benefit for long-distance families trying to navigate the maze of paperwork and laws for moving mortal remains.

Once you settle on the final arrangements, you need to decide who will take charge of the estate—and this is probably *the single most important decision* you will make when a loved one dies.

If you choose a professional executor, you can have peace of mind knowing that your loved one's assets will be managed efficiently—and that you've just saved yourself a year or two of headaches, stress, and potentially expensive travel.

An insider's secret about heirs and professional executors...*you always have a choice.*

You might think if there's a named executor in the will, your hands are tied—the decision is made for you. Or, if there's no will, you might assume you have to go with whomever the court appoints.

But that's just not the case. Heirs can *always* override those appointments, as long as they're in agreement. And no one *loses* a thing.

EXAMPLE: When Mrs. Zhou died in New York without a will, state intestacy law divided her estate among her three sisters, two of whom lived in China, while the third, Joy, lived nearby in Philadelphia. As the only U.S. heir, Joy was first in line to be executor under state law, but she didn't really want the job and hesitated about accepting her role with the court. Her own daughter had just had a baby, and her sisters in China were already voicing concerns that Joy would favor herself when she settled the estate.

Joy had heard of professional executors—a friend from church had used one when her father died in California. But Joy thought she would either have to give up her share of the estate if she resigned her job as executor, or pay the executor's fees out of her own share.

When the cacophony of concerned calls and texts from her sisters became too much to bear, Joy called a professional executor in New York just to ask a few questions. When she learned that using a professional wouldn't affect her share of the estate at all, she decided on the spot it was the perfect solution.

When she explained the idea to her sisters, they jumped onboard immediately. Joy was able to avoid the onerous job and spend her spare time with her new grandchild, and her sisters were reassured that everything would be handled fairly.

CHOOSING A PROFESSIONAL EXECUTOR IF YOU'RE WRITING YOUR WILL

Professional executors take the stress off your family members or friends, and give you peace of mind that your estate will be handled competently. You can name a professional executor in your will instead of choosing a family member or friend to avoid any conflict.

When you're ready to choose a professional executor, there are a few things to keep in mind:

- The attorney drafting your will is a great source of recommendations for a good professional executor. Ask for referrals—but be sure to vet them before you include them in your will.
- If your estate has unusual elements (see the list above), ask about the executor's experience in those areas.
- Age is a big deal. If you choose an executor 20 or 30 years older than you, odds are he may not be alive when you die.

Talk to the attorney who drafted your will about naming a

successor. Some states even let your executor name a successor. You can get around a lot of issues if you nail down succession in your will.

KEY TAKEAWAYS

- Heirs aren't stuck with a court-appointed executor or the person named in the will. You always have the option to choose a professional executor.
- Heirs don't lose anything by hiring a professional executor; your share of the estate is exactly the same.
- Professional executors are the best choice when you're dealing with a multinational estate or an estate with unusual assets.

CHAPTER 7

PROFESSIONAL EXECUTOR FEES

IN MOST AREAS OF LIFE, it's considerably more expensive to hire a professional than to do a job yourself. Not so when it comes to hiring a professional executor. This is the rare situation when hiring a pro costs the same—and possibly even a lot less—than muddling through on your own.

That's because executor fees are set by state law, so the estate pays the same amount *no matter who does the job*.

Choosing a professional executor could actually save money on legal and CPA fees. Think about it: if your niece Susie settles the estate, she'll consult lawyers and accountants and financial professionals a lot more often than a professional executor who handles estate issues every day.

And when it comes to preserving estate assets and conserving its resources, a professional executor almost always does it better. A professional executor knows how to get things done efficiently at the lowest cost. He won't make bad decisions that lower the value of the estate or fritter away money on unnecessary fees the way an amateur might.

HOW EXECUTOR FEES ARE CALCULATED

Executor fees vary depending on where the estate is settled. Most states set the executor fee as a percentage of the total value of the estate, while others set an hourly rate and ask the executor to keep a record of his hours.

In New York and California, executor fees are written into probate law. The New York executor fee schedule looks like this:

- 5% of the first $100,000 received and paid out
- 4% of amounts received and paid out of the next $200,000
- 3% of amounts received and paid out between $300,001 and $1,000,000
- 2.5% of amounts received and paid out between $1,000,001 and $5,000,000
- 2% of all amounts in excess of $5,000,000

EXAMPLE: When Mrs. Lemieux's estate was finally settled, the executor had liquidated assets and paid out expenses, including disbursements to the heirs, totaling $500,000. The executor fees came to $19,000 by New York state law ($5,000 on the first $100,000 + $8,000 on the next $200,000 + $6,000 for the remaining $200,000 = $19,000.) Regardless of whether Cousin Millie or a professional executor settled the estate, the estate would pay $19,000.

Although the fees initially seemed high to the heirs, in comparison to the 6% commission on the sale of Mrs. Lemieux's $375,000 house ($22,500), the professional executor's fees seemed more than reasonable for a year or two of work.

And if the estate is settled in a state that pays by the hour, who do you think would take more time—an inexperienced family member muddling her way through, or a professional executor who knows exactly what needs to be done? In an hourly-rate state, using a professional executor is almost always the most economical choice.

FAMILY MEMBERS AND EXECUTOR FEES

There's a catch-22 when it comes to paying family members for serving as executor. There's an expectation among family members that Aunt Beth or Cousin David would never—*should never*— accept executor fees because they're part of the family and it's like stealing from the heirs.

On the other hand, Aunt Beth or Cousin David know they are going to spend a lot of time and effort on the job and deserve to be paid.

If they accept the money, the other family members may perceive it as an act of disloyalty to their loved one. If they turn it down, the executor could feel as though the family is taking unfair advantage—and may not give the estate their best effort.

If the executor is a beneficiary and succumbs to family pressure to waive her fee, not only is she not getting paid for all the work she does, she is in effect giving the free-riders an unearned bonus. Ultimately, any unpaid expenses (including executor fees) increase the value of the estate when it's divided among the heirs at settlement.

EXAMPLE: The executor fees for Mr. Bing's estate came out to $33,000. His daughter Danielle was the named executor, and the will divided the estate equally between Danielle and her two sisters. Danielle was persuaded to waive her executor fee, so that $33,000 remained part of the estate. When Danielle finally settled the estate, each of her sisters got an additional $11,000 in their inheritance checks (one-third of $33,000) even though they'd done none of the hard work required to settle their father's final affairs.

WHEN IS THE EXECUTOR PAID?

Many families believe they have to pay out of pocket to hire an executor—that they have to come up with the executor fee upfront.

Not true. The executor is paid at the *end* of the settlement process—whether the executor is a family member or a pro. The heirs pay nothing out of pocket to hire a professional executor.

Heirs may have certain expenses not related to the executor —copies of death certificates, fees for a probate lawyer, for example—that they pay when the expenses occur, but executor fees are deducted from the estate at settlement.

Some courts allow executors to be paid at certain benchmarks in the settlement process, but most professional executors know when they accept a case that they won't get paid for a year or more.

Non-professional executors, on the other hand, are usually surprised by that fact. Many believe they get their money as soon as they are duly appointed by the court. When they find out it may be *years* before they get paid, they often lose their motivation for the job.

If costs are keeping you from hiring a professional executor, you're looking at it the wrong way. The estate pays the same amount no matter who does the job—and you and the other heirs pay nothing upfront to get the services of an experienced pro to settle your loved one's estate.

ARE THERE FEES FOR NAMING A PROFESSIONAL EXECUTOR IN MY WILL?

Executors become eligible for state-mandated executor fees only after they've been duly appointed by the court to serve in that role. There is no cost to naming a professional executor in your will.

One exception, however: if you're writing your will and you decide you'd like a consultation with your professional executor before you make a decision on who to choose, you may be billed at the executor's hourly rate. Fortunately, most people don't require an initial consultation to know whether or not a particular professional executor is a good fit.

KEY TAKEAWAYS

- Executor fees are set by state law, usually as a percentage of the estate.
- The estate pays exactly the same amount whether you use a professional executor or a family member or friend.
- You don't pay an executor anything upfront—the executor gets paid when the estate is settled.

CHAPTER 8

PROFESSIONAL EXECUTOR FAQS

HIRING a professional executor is a straightforward process, but it's normal to have questions. This chapter deals with some of the most common. It's arranged in two sections: the first for families facing the death of a loved one, and the second for those writing or updating their wills.

WHEN SOMEONE HAS DIED

My mother named me the executor in her will, but I'd rather hire a professional executor. Is that allowed?

As long as the heirs consent, naming a new executor is a simple matter of signing some court documents. The only potential stumbling block is the unanimous agreement of the heirs. This is usually not a problem, however, once you explain it won't cost the estate anything extra to turn the job over to a professional.

If I'm the named executor, shouldn't I honor my loved one's wishes? I feel bad backing out.

Professional executors hear this one *a lot,* but the fact is, few people, when they write their will, really understand what they're asking of their loved ones. If they did, they might not impose the job on a friend or family member.

You shouldn't feel bad about hiring a professional executor —he will honor your loved one's wishes as well as (if not better than) you would yourself. As a person with no legal or tax background and no experience settling an estate, you will have a much more difficult time managing the process, and may even make a few unintentional mistakes along the way.

A great way to honor your loved one's wishes is to ensure the heirs get the assets and gifts accumulated for them over the years quickly and competently. Settling an estate can be a very long, drawn-out process. If you hire a professional executor, the heirs generally get paid much more quickly.

Finally, many executors grow to resent the role they were given as it consumes ever more of their time and emotional resources. Turning the job over to a professional means your memories of your loved one won't be tarnished by bad feelings.

I just found out about professional executors and I want to hire one, but I've already been appointed by the court. Now what?

It's definitely more difficult, but certainly not impossible.

There are court costs that go along with removing an executor and replacing her with a professional. Depending on where you are in the process, however, the costs may be worth it.

If you've only recently been appointed—if you're only three months or so into what could easily be an 18-month process, the cost-benefit analysis is a little more clear. You are saving yourself a year or more of aggravation. The court costs are a small price to pay for reclaiming a year of your life.

Should the estate have two executors?

This comes up a lot with families who think it would be a good idea to have a family member *and* a professional executor, just so the family is "represented." It's *usually* a bad idea to have more than one executor—on multiple levels.

First, executors must act in unison. This isn't only a matter of agreement between the two executors (which can be hard enough sometimes), but it's also a matter of logistics. If there are two executors, then you will need two signatures on every document, two people present for every bank meeting, court hearing, real estate closing...you get the idea.

And when executors disagree? The court gets involved to settle the dispute, costing the estate money and drawing out the settlement process.

If you hire a professional executor, he is legally bound to represent the estate and act in its best interests; you don't need a family member to oversee him. Remember, if the heirs believe the executor is negligent in his duties, they can file for damages against him in court. It's a win-win situation for the heirs.

I live abroad but I need a professional executor for a U.S. estate. Do I have to meet with the executor before I hire him?

There's no need to meet with your professional executor—why complicate a simple matter with a costly international trip? If you do your research and you feel comfortable with the executor you choose, it's a matter you can easily manage from home. You'll need to sign some court documents, but the professional executor will coordinate that for you.

The next chapter includes tips for choosing a good professional executor, and the steps to take when you're ready to hire one, if you're looking for more information.

WHEN YOU'RE WRITING YOUR WILL

Should I name two executors in my will?

You *can,* but as mentioned above, it's generally a bad idea. If you're inclined to name two family members or your two best friends, you're setting them up for disaster. If family members or friends have a falling-out as executors, it's not just the estate that suffers—long-standing relationships can be destroyed. It's best to choose just one person as the executor.

If you're nominating a professional executor, there's no need to add a second family member or friend to watch out for your interests—for all the reasons mentioned above. The professional executor will faithfully carry out your wishes.

I think I want to hire a professional executor, but what if I change my mind?

If you name a professional executor in your will, and you later decide you want to use a family member—or even another professional executor—just update your will with the new executor's name. You aren't making a lifetime commitment when you appoint a professional executor in your will.

And professional executors won't force themselves into a situation where they aren't wanted. For example, if Mr. Brown nominates a professional executor in his will, but after his death, his wife wants to handle his affairs on her own, a competent executor will readily step aside.

I don't want a non-family member to have control over who gets what in my estate. Can a professional executor change the terms of my will?

A professional executor is legally bound to carry out your wishes as expressed in your will, or according to state intestacy laws if there is no valid will. The executor can't change beneficiaries, alter your bequests, or do anything with your assets that runs contrary to your will or state law.

If you are worried about how your estate will be divided after your death, there is absolutely *no* advantage in naming a family member over a professional executor. In fact, in theory, a professional executor is *more* likely to honor your wishes exactly than a family member might be, because he is detached from the situation. He won't be swayed by family conflict or high emotions; he'll settle your estate exactly as you direct in your will.

Does a professional executor have to sign my will?

As with international families hiring a U.S. executor, there's no reason for you to meet your executor in person. He doesn't need to sign your will—once you nominate a professional executor, you can simply have your lawyer send him a copy of your will for his records.

Of course, if you *want* to meet with him before you write or update your will, you certainly can. But once your will is written, you only need to check in with your professional executor whenever you update your will to make sure he's still available.

What happens if the executor dies before I do?

Most professional executors have a formal succession plan to handle situations like this. New York state law requires one, in fact. If the professional executor named in your will dies or becomes disabled, he must have a designated "transition attorney" who will help you transfer to another executor of your choice.

How do I know if I made the right choice for my professional executor?

If you've done some research and chosen an executor you're

comfortable with, you shouldn't have reason to worry. Although choosing your executor *seems* like a very weighty life decision, it's really not—for a number of reasons.

Most people live for decades after writing a will. In all likelihood, unless you're approaching the end of your life, the person you choose today will probably *not* be the person settling your estate when you eventually die. The idea behind naming a professional executor in your will *today* is to know that you have a reliable contingency plan in place should something happen to you in the next five to ten years.

Finally, naming a professional executor in your will doesn't necessarily bind your heirs. If your surviving spouse doesn't want to use your named executor, an ethical executor will readily step down. Given the personal liability involved, no executor will force himself into a situation in which he isn't wanted. In other words, it's not an irrevocable decision.

How is the professional executor notified?

The professional executor's contact information is generally contained in the will. Either the lawyer who drafted the will contacts your executor, or a family member with a copy of the will gets in touch. The executor already has a copy of the will, so once he's notified of the death, he can take it from there.

KEY TAKEAWAYS

- If you want to hire a professional executor, it's best to do it before the named executor is appointed—although it's still possible after the named executor is certified by the court.
- Naming, or appointing, two executors is almost always a bad idea: you don't need a family member to oversee a professional executor.
- It's not necessary to have a face-to-face appointment with a professional executor to hire him—the executor can coordinate the court documents for you.

CHAPTER 9

NEXT STEPS: HOW TO WORK WITH US

IF YOU'RE ready to hire a professional executor, your first step is to choose the right one for your family's situation. In the next section, I'll describe how our office works to help you decide if we're a good fit.

I'll start with some basic information about our firm.

WHERE WE WORK

We work primarily with estates in New York, especially if there is real estate involved. If there is no real estate, we consider out-of-state estates on a case-by-case basis.

We do a lot of work with international estates in which the deceased lived overseas but owned assets such as a bank or brokerage account in the U.S. New York is an ideal base for managing international estates for many reasons, not the least of which is its status as an international financial center. Most major banks and financial institutions maintain a presence in New York, so we are well-positioned to handle situations arising from international assets.

In addition, New York has a robust and sophisticated judicial system; the courts are experienced in dealing with international estate matters. Other jurisdictions may have fewer legal professionals who handle international estates, and that lack of experience may draw out the settlement process.

SPECIFIC EXPERIENCE

Just because someone has a law degree doesn't mean he has the background or specific estate experience you need in a professional executor. The nitty-gritty details aren't part of the law school curriculum—competence comes from actually settling many, *many* estates.

My staff and I have acted as professional executor or trustee for over 250 estates over the course of my 20-year career, and we've probated hundreds more. There's not much we haven't seen when it comes to estates, so few things take us by surprise.

ANTHONY'S SKILL STACK

My educational and professional background gives me an ideal set of skills and experiences for professional executorship. I worked my way through law school at an accounting firm and owned an H&R Block tax franchise for several years. I have legal and practical tax experience when it comes to filing tax returns for estates or deceased individuals—and knowing when to bring in estate tax pros (and how to review their work).

Most estates involve real estate, and I've handled hundreds of real estate deals—many times as a professional executor. And if your loved one's property is in New York, you *definitely* need experience. The New York real estate market is complex, especially if there's a condo or co-op involved. I authored a best-selling book on the subject of real estate with specific sections on the New York market.

Does your loved one's estate involve a business or partnership interest? I'm a seasoned entrepreneur myself—I launched a renewable energy manufacturing company in East Africa (so I'm intimately familiar with the complicated issues involved in international business), owned a retail franchise, and manage my own law practice, which includes paralegals and support staff.

Publishing, technology, copyright issues—that's in my wheelhouse, too. I've self-published best-selling books on personal finance and money management, and I'm a prolific YouTuber and podcaster. I make it easy for you to get to know me by my books, blogs, video, and podcasts so you don't have to wonder who you're hiring or if I have the experience you're looking for in a professional executor.

OUR TEAM

You *can* hire a solo attorney as your professional executor, but it's better to have an experienced team managing your estate. That way, all the details are handled as efficiently and cost-effectively as possible.

I have several paralegals who specialize in different aspects of estate work. One, for example, handles all court documents and filings. Another focuses on estate administration —dealing with banks, government agencies, and the IRS. A third coordinates the settlement processes so everything stays on track and moves along smoothly. We're a very efficient team—can you imagine how different it would be managing it all on your own?

In addition, I have a network of lawyers in various specialties to handle any legal work that comes up during settlement. It's surprising how many legal problems can be associated with an estate—a tenant who needs to be evicted, a lawsuit to collect from a business creditor, a mortgage foreclosure to defend. For every situation, I have the right attorney who is equipped to best conserves the estate's assets.

Estates have many moving parts—taxes, real estate closings, even cleaning out a home or office. My network includes every type of professional who might be required to settle your estate.

MINIMUM ESTATE SIZE

We work with estates valued at $250,000 or more, with at least $25,000 in liquid assets (bank accounts, brokerage accounts, life insurance policies).

A WORD ABOUT OUR INTERNATIONAL ESTATE EXPERIENCE

A significant portion of our executorship cases involve international estates; it's become one of our specialties. We handle estates for clients all over the world and we have a lot of experience with the different legal, financial, and tax issues that go along with international estates.

It's a side of our practice we really enjoy—getting to know and help people from around the world. If you have international estate issues, we have the experience and professional network to settle them quickly and efficiently.

GET TO KNOW US

It's easy to learn more about me and my practice in your preferred way and at your convenience.

- Check out the videos on my YouTube channel (http://www.youtube.com/c/anthonyspark)

- Listen to my podcast, *Simple Money Wins*, on iTunes and other podcast platforms

- Read my best-selling books, available on Amazon

(https://www.amazon.com/Anthony-S.-Park/e/B07KY2JDGR)

You'll notice we really focus on your convenience and accessibility. We don't think you should have to schedule a phone consultation or face-to-face meeting to know whether we're the right team for you.

If you have any questions along the way, please feel free to email or text our office. If we see the same question pop up frequently, we may even post the answer on our website or address it in one of our podcasts.

HIRING ANTHONY WHEN SOMEONE HAS DIED

Laura and her brothers were with their father when he died in a New York hospice. She knew she was the executor of her father's will, so she immediately set to work getting the death certificates and other documents in order. She set up an appointment with her father's lawyer to get a copy of the will and find out her next steps.

As Mr. Carpenter, the attorney, explained the process, Laura realized with dismay there was no way she could do the job from her home in Seattle. She asked Mr. Carpenter if there was any way she could get out of it, and what would happen if she refused to serve as executor. Mr. Carpenter brought up hiring a professional executor based in New York—and Laura immediately saw the advantages. The problem, as she saw it, was getting her brothers to buy into the idea.

Her brother Thomas, who lived in the British Virgin Islands, embraced the idea; he knew he couldn't take over the task. Her other brother David, however, lived in New York and didn't understand why he shouldn't serve instead. Once Laura told him what was involved, and explained that a professional executor wouldn't cost them any money out of their own pockets, he quickly signed on.

If you want to hire us to handle your loved one's estate, the process is very simple.

(1) Email us at executor@anthonyspark.com or call our office at 212-401-2990 with some basic information—name, state, date of death—so we can do a conflicts check.

(2) If everything looks good, we'll be in touch to gather more detailed information and documents, including the will, death certificate, and estimate of estate assets.

(3) If we're a good fit, we'll send you some court documents to sign to get started.

Ours is an end-to-end service that completely frees you from all estate details. Once you return your court documents, your only job is to sit back and wait for the FedEx package containing your inheritance check. It really is *that* simple.

HIRING ANTHONY WHEN YOU'RE WRITING YOUR WILL

When Jordan's wife gave birth to twins, he knew it was time to do the responsible thing and make a will. He struggled with who to name as executor—his wife would have her hands full with two babies and he knew he didn't want her to have the burden of settling his estate in the event something happened to him.

Jordan considered naming his father, but chances were good his father would die long before he did. His brother lived thousands of miles away in Alaska, so he wasn't a viable choice, either. His sister lived nearby, but he knew she wouldn't appreciate the job. Ultimately, he decided a professional executor was the best choice.

If you're writing your will and want to hire our office as professional executor, it's a very straightforward process.

(1) Email us at executor@anthonyspark.com or text our office at 212-401-2990 with some basic information. We'll do a conflicts check to make sure we can ethically accept your case.

(2) If everything checks out, we'll ask for a copy of your will and some information on estate assets to make sure we're a good fit.

(3) Once we give you the go-ahead, have your lawyer write us into your will and email us a final copy for our files.

That's all you need to do to have the peace of mind that comes from knowing a professional executor is available to step in for your family.

KEY TAKEAWAYS

- You don't need a face-to-face meeting to hire me as your professional executor—in fact, we prefer emails or texts to keep it simple and cheap.
- You pay nothing upfront to hire me to settle a loved one's estate or serve as the executor of your will.
- My talent stack is uniquely suited to professional executorship—in addition to handling hundreds of estates, I've also got accounting, real estate, international business, and entrepreneurship in my background. Whatever's in your loved one's estate, I'm prepared to manage it efficiently.

IF YOU LIKED THIS BOOK...

Thanks for reading. If you enjoyed this book, I'd appreciate a short review. Please consider leaving your honest review on Amazon or your favorite store.

And join my email list for new book announcements: https://anthonyspark.com/join

ABOUT THE AUTHOR

Anthony is a New York executor, attorney, and entrepreneur. Anthony's cases have been featured in many places, including the *Wall Street Journal*, *New York Times*, CNBC, and *MarketWatch*.

Anthony also hosts the popular podcast *Simple Money Wins* (available on YouTube, iTunes, and anthonyspark.com).

How to Buy Your Perfect First Home: What Every First-Time Homebuyer Needs to Know

How Probate Works: A Guide for Executors, Heirs, and Families

How to Get Promoted: Simple Steps to Better Title and Higher Pay

How to Invest for Retirement: A Simple Path to Retiring Rich, Independent, and Free

The Solo Ager Estate Plan: Trust and Estate Essentials for Single, Childless Seniors

INDEX